D0712970

IT'S TRUE! Pigs Do Fly

Other  titles

Terry Denton
PICTURES BY Terry Denton

IT'S TRUE! Pigs Do Fly

annick press
toronto + new york + vancouver

For Otto Lilienthal, my hero

Copyright © text Terry Denton 2006
Copyright © illustrations Terry Denton 2006
Series design copyright © Ruth Grüner 2006

Annick Press Ltd.
First published in Australia by Allen & Unwin.

We acknowledge the support of the Canada Council for the Arts,
the Ontario Arts Council, and the Government of Canada through
the Book Publishing Industry Development Program (BPIDP)
for our publishing activities.

Proofread by Elizabeth McLean
Production of this edition by Antonia Banyard
Cover photograph: Getty Images
Set in 12.5pt Minion by Ruth Grüner

Cataloging in Publication

Denton, Terry
It's true! pigs do fly / written and illustrated by Terry Denton. —
North American ed.

Includes bibliographical references and index.
ISBN-13: 978-1-55037-949-5 (bound).— ISBN-10: 1-55037-949-6 (bound)
ISBN-13: 978-1-55037-948-8 (pbk.).— ISBN-10: 1-55037-948-8 (pbk.)

1. Flight—History—Juvenile literature. 2. Aeronautics—
History—Juvenile literature. I. Title.
TL547.D45 2006   j629.13'09   C2005-906226-6

Printed in Canada

1 3 5 7 9 10 8 6 4 2

Published in the U.S.A. by
Annick Press (U.S.) Ltd.

Distributed in Canada by:
Firefly Books Ltd.
66 Leek Crescent
Richmond Hill, ON
L4B 1H1

Distributed in the U.S.A. by:
Firefly Books (U.S.) Inc.
P.O. Box 1338
Ellicott Station
Buffalo, NY 14205

Visit our website at: www.annickpress.com

CONTENTS

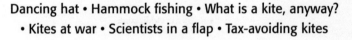

Why Flight?

When I was a young child, I sat in church pretending to pray like everyone else. But really I was looking up at the paintings of angels flying around the ceiling. I wanted to fly just like them.

Later, Superman became my hero. And still later, my fantasy was to soar like a bird over a wild surf beach, or hang high like an eagle over a wilderness valley.

Then, one magical day in my early thirties, I really did fly for the first time—in an airplane. As I looked down on the world, I thought, "Earth is good, but sky is better." I suppose it's the sense of freedom that I like. Not having to be held to the ground by gravity.

Birds are so lucky!

Pigs do fly!

Take a look at that pig above! Compared to a bird, it is round, heavy and very chunky. No matter how hard it might flap its little feet, that pig will never fly.

Yet, whenever I look at a jumbo jet struggling down a tarmac, I think ... "Flying pig! There is no way this round, heavy and very cumbersome jet plane will ever take off." But amazingly it does. This big white "pig" lumbers into the air and, once free of gravity, it soars like the most majestic eagle.

So how does such a big, lumpy thing get off the ground? And how did humans learn to fly? That is the story of this book. And it all started a couple of thousand years ago with the invention of the humble kite.

Chapter 1

As high as a kite

Dancing hat

Imagine you are in China, about 2000 years ago. There is a farmer working in a field on a very windy day. His hat keeps blowing off and he has to chase it across the field.

"Stupid hat! Stupid wind!!" he says angrily.

When the farmer catches his hat, he stomps back to the veggie plot and places it very carefully on the ground again.

But as soon as he returns to work, the wind blows and his hat flies up into the air again.

"You stupid wind!" he curses. "Leave my hat alone."

Then he has a bright idea. This time he ties a string to his hat and ties the other end of the string to a bush.

"Now I have you beaten, Mr. Wind."

When the wind blows again, the hat flies up into the air. Held back by the string, it hovers just above him. The farmer is amused at his hat dancing. He lets out more string. His hat flies higher and higher.

All the other farmers join him, laughing at the flying hat. They all beg for a turn holding the string. They may have been the world's first kite-flyers.

Hammock fishing

Another story tells of a man lying in a hammock on a beach on a Pacific Island. He sips milk out of a coconut. His family sits nearby. This man is hard at work, fishing!

He holds onto a line. Only the line isn't set in the water. Instead it goes straight up in the air. Is he fishing in the air? For seagulls, maybe?

On the end of his long line a kite hovers way out over the sea. The kite is made from large leaves sewn together, and hanging off it is a baited fishing line, way out in the deep water where the best fish are.

The fisherman is lying in his hammock fishing, and he doesn't even have to get wet. Very clever, eh? That's what I call good technology!

What is a kite, anyway?

Kites have been around such a long time that no one really knows when and where they actually originated. Flying hats and simple leaf kites might have marked the beginning of man's long quest to unlock the mysteries of flight.

DIAMOND KITE

TUBE KITE

BOX KITE

FIGHTING KITE

Kites around the world come in many shapes and sizes. There are diamond-shaped kites, box kites, tube kites, fighting kites and many more.

Every kite consists of a light frame covered with even lighter fabric or paper. They are usually flown at the end of a long string. They often have tails.

A kite can't just leap into the sky by itself, it needs a wind.

5

The string pulls the kite against the wind, causing it to push the wind downwards. The wind pushes back against the kite with a force that equals the pull of the string.

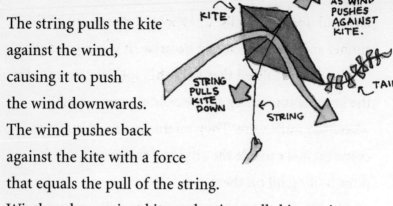

Wind pushes against kite and string pulls kite against wind, so the kite stays in the air. The tail helps to keep it balanced. And Bob's your uncle, the kite flies.[1]

Kites at war

One of the first uses of kites was in warfare. They helped a Chinese general, Han Hsin, to conquer a city. He was attacking the enemy walls, but the siege was not going so well. The walls were too high and too strong for his army.

Then Hsin thought of a cunning plan. He ordered his men to dig a long tunnel from their camp up to the

[1] Even if Bob is your aunt, the kite will still fly.

6

city and under its walls. They would storm out of the tunnel and take the city by surprise. It was a good plan!

But Hsin realized that while his soldiers were under the ground tunnelling they wouldn't know exactly where the walls were. They might make a mistake and come up just outside the city, and the enemy would pour boiling oil on them.

He didn't want his men to simply walk up to the walls with a measuring tape. That would give away their plan. And besides, the enemy would pour more boiling oil over them.

"Go fly a kite!" General Hsin ordered his men.

And they did, letting out enough string so the kite was flying just above the walls of the city. Then they hauled the kite back in and measured the string. It was an easy matter then to work out the distance to the walls.

The soldiers tunnelled the right distance and emerged inside the city, surprising their enemy, who were probably too busy boiling oil.

So a powerful city was defeated by a flimsy kite, and by the cunning of General Hsin.

Kites have also been used in warfare for signalling and communication. Imagine two units of the same army camped a few kilometers (a couple of miles) apart with their enemy in between. They need to talk to each other, but they don't have radios. It's 500 AD in China and radios haven't been invented yet. So they fly kites of different colors and patterns. These have different meanings that can be read like marine flags.

By flying the kites very high, the armies can communicate over very long distances. It's a bit like the smoke signals used by the Native Americans.

Who needs a telephone?

During World War I (1914–1918) the British, French, Italian and Russian armies all still used kites for enemy observation and signalling. But with the introduction of airplanes, kites quickly became outdated.

Scientists in a flap

Kites first arrived in Europe from China in the 1300s. The Venetian adventurer Marco Polo brought them back from one of his many journeys. At first they were only used as playthings.

In the 1700s, scientists started attaching their instruments to kites and sending them to heights that were never before possible. Kites helped people learn a great deal about clouds, wind and weather patterns.

In the 1740s, Benjamin Franklin was into extreme science. During thunderstorms he would rush outside and fly his kite, hoping it would get struck by lightning. Eventually he was able to prove the link between lightning and electricity. Without the kite he would never have succeeded.

CRASH!!

The early pioneers of aviation—George Cayley, Otto Lilienthal, Samuel Langley, the Wright Brothers and Lawrence Hargrave—all began their research by experimenting with kites.

Tax-avoiding kites

Over the years, there were some weird people who put kites to strange uses. None was weirder than Englishman George Pocock.

In the 1820s many roads were toll roads. There were no cars in those days, just horses and carriages, so tolls were charged on the number of horses hitched up to a carriage.

George Pocock hated paying road tolls. So he hatched a brilliant, but slightly crazy, plan to avoid these tolls.

He replaced the horses on his carriage with a huge pair of kites. On windy days they would pull his carriage along the tollway at about 30 kilometers (20 miles) per hour. In a really big wind he could get it up to 100 kilometers (60 miles) per hour.

A carriage without horses couldn't be charged any tolls, so George was able to travel the roads free of charge. The main drawback was that he could only take his carriage out on windy days. Poor George!

Although kites were useful in many ways, inventors realized they could never be capable of long, controlled and powered flight. Many believed the future of flight lay with ornithopters, machines that imitated the way birds fly.

Chapter 2

Make like a bird

Leonardo da Vinci is well known for his painting of the Mona Lisa. But the famous artist was also an inventor who was crazy about flight. Or maybe just crazy!

In the 1400s he spent many hours studying birds and other flying creatures. He believed that the best way for humans to fly was to imitate flapping flight. Creatures that get around using flapping flight, like birds and insects, make up two-thirds of all creatures on Earth.

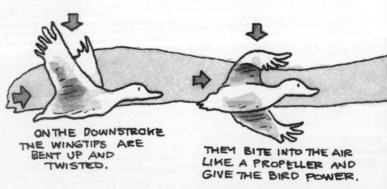

ON THE DOWNSTROKE THE WINGTIPS ARE BENT UP AND TWISTED.

THEY BITE INTO THE AIR LIKE A PROPELLER AND GIVE THE BIRD POWER.

The bones of a bird's wing are hollow. This helps it fly by keeping its weight to a minimum. For its weight, a bird is amazingly strong.

Unfortunately, humans are the opposite. We're heavy and weak, making it almost impossible for us to fly like a bird. To succeed in flapping flight, a human would need really huge wings, two to three times longer than our arms, but unfortunately we would never have the strength to flap them.

With winders, ropes and pulleys, Leonardo set about designing many complex machines that imitated this flapping flight. They were called ornithopters. They usually had a pilot strapped into the middle of a wooden frame surrounded by huge, silk-covered wooden wings.

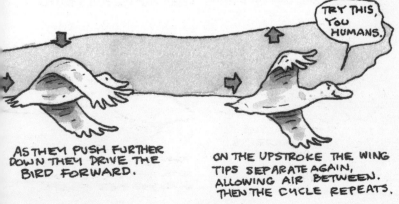

AS THEY PUSH FURTHER DOWN THEY DRIVE THE BIRD FORWARD.

ON THE UPSTROKE THE WING TIPS SEPARATE AGAIN, ALLOWING AIR BETWEEN. THEN THE CYCLE REPEATS.

Leonardo didn't have the strong, lightweight materials that we have today, like titanium, Kevlar and carbon fiber. Instead he had to use what was around at the time, so his lightest ornithopter would have weighed about 300 kilograms (660 pounds). That's about the weight of two couches,[1] or four fully grown female gorillas, or half a manatee!

[1] Two 150-kilogram (330-pound) couches, that is!

We are lucky Leonardo was too busy inventing other things to fly one of his ornithopters. He would never have been able to keep his wings flapping and would have crashed to his death and then we would never have had the beautiful Mona Lisa to adore.

Through the ages, many extreme inventors have built and flown machines similar to Leonardo's designs. Few flew; most plummeted. Amazingly, despite this high death toll, inventors refused to give up on the ornithopter idea. There were still madmen building them as late as the 1930s.

Micro-mechanical flappers

Today, in various parts of the world, scientists are again working on ornithopters.

During the 1990s a group of Russian scientists built a full-sized manned ornithopter, which took off with the help of a small motorcycle engine and then continued to fly under human power at heights of 10–12 meters (33–40 feet).

Despite this, most researchers have been trying to develop miniature ornithopters, like the Berkeley Micromechanical Flying Insect, which weighs a mere 100 milligrams (.0035 ounce). Another research group,

UH, OH.

called Aerovironment, has built a tiny 12-gram (1/3 ounce) ornithopter, which runs on a battery-powered vibrator motor from a cell phone. It is the size of a small bird, with a 23-centimeter (9-inch) wingspan,[2] and can fly for up to 20 minutes at speeds of about 24 kilometers (15 miles) per hour. The people at Aerovironment imagine fitting it with a camera and using it for environmental and military purposes.

The successes of today's ornithopter researchers are only possible because of 21st-century technology and materials. Inventors in the 1700s had no such miracle materials to work with. As a result, they were frustrated by their constant failures and finally gave up on flapping flight. Some returned to kites instead and tried to develop heavier-than-air fixed-wing gliders. Others saw the future in lighter-than-air craft, and that is the path we will explore next.

CRASH!!

[2] A little bit bigger than this book is high.

BALLOON

FLAME

BOWL

THIS WILL END IN TEARS

Chapter 3

A lot of hot air

Bart's balloon

One day in 1709, the king and queen of Portugal were sitting around in their palace, when a strange guy knocked on their door.

"I am Bartolomeu de Gusmao of Brazil," he announced. "And I have something earth-shatteringly brilliant to show you."

So the king and queen called all their friends and relatives and hangers-on into the palace. Bartolomeu de Gusmao removed from his backpack a ball of paper. He opened it out into a sphere about half a meter (1½ feet) in diameter. He attached a small bowl at the bottom.

18

Then he crumpled up some paper into the bowl and set fire to it.

A few seconds later, the paper sphere and bowl shot up into the air. Everyone gasped in amazement. As far as we know, they were the first people to ever see a hot-air balloon.[1]

Then someone started screaming. Panic! The hot-air balloon had crashed into the curtains, setting them alight.

Eventually, someone put the fire out. Oddly enough, the king and queen were not worried about their precious curtains. In fact, they were delighted. And Bart of Brazil had become an instant hero.

Who was to know in 1709 that this hot-air balloon was to mark the beginning of something really big? Almost 200 years later, people would be flying in heavier-than-air planes powered by gas engines. And Bartolomeu de Gusmao of Brazil had lit the fire that started the whole thing.

[1] Except Bartolomeu. And his family. And most of his village. And probably half of Brazil.

The Montgolfiers do the washing

Not a lot happened in the hot-air balloon business until 73 years later.

In a house in the French countryside, two brothers called Joseph and Étienne Montgolfier were washing their clothes. Good boys!

Doesn't sound very exciting, does it? But in the world of invention, really important breakthroughs often come from simple, unimportant events.

Joseph Montgolfier hung his shirt over a clotheshorse to dry in front of the fire. The light silk shirt billowed and lifted slightly. Joseph and Étienne were amazed. Maybe they had seen this happen a hundred times before and never really thought much about it. But this day, for some reason, it caught their attention.

Now you or I would have been distracted immediately by some stupid show on TV and forgotten about the shirt thing altogether. But in 1782 Joseph and Étienne didn't have any TV. Were they poor? No, TV just hadn't been invented yet.

So the Montgolfiers had no choice but to watch their shirt. They realized that the hot air from the fire must be making the shirt rise. But how?

Suddenly Joseph and Étienne started thinking a lot about hot air. Boys do that.[2]

A real whopper

Joseph Montgolfier was a bit of a simple country boy. He had wandered in and out of school and various jobs before settling down to study law. He was a dreamer who loved tinkering and fiddling around with mechanical things. His brother Étienne was a rich businessman who managed their father's paper-making factory. He was a good engineer, brilliant at figuring

[2] Not *that* kind of hot air, though!

out detailed problems. They made an ideal partnership. And best of all for balloon experimenters, they had all the paper they could ever want!

The brothers spent the next few months making paper balloons, filling them with hot air and watching them fly. If one balloon succeeded they would try building a bigger one. If that flew, then an even bigger one! Until eventually they built a real whopper, measuring 10 meters (33 feet) in diameter. That's nearly three times as wide as your average bedroom.

When they filled this balloon with hot air, it immediately lifted off the ground with such force that their four helpers who were trying to hold it down almost went up with it. If they hadn't let go of the ropes, they would have been the first men to fly.[3]

SHARP-BEAKED BIRD FLYING TOWARD BALLOON

JOSEPH MONTGOLFIER BRINGING MORE FUEL

[3] And probably the first airmen to die.

22

23

The balloon flew down the road and across a few fields and landed in a nearby farm, scaring a farmer and his cows half to death.

After that success the brothers decided that the time was right for a grand and public demonstration of their amazing hot-air balloon. The brothers Montgolfier decided to build their biggest balloon yet for a test flight before the officials of the very wealthy, very important king of France.

How does a balloon work?

You may be wondering how a hot-air balloon works. I have two answers to this question:

Answer number one: It just does, okay? If you are happy with that answer, then you can flip forward to the next page. If you are not satisfied, then try . . .

Answer number two: The balloon is full of cool air, which the fire heats to about 100° Celsius (212° Fahrenheit). When the air heats, it expands. Now there is not enough room in the balloon for all that air, so some air is pushed out of the bottom of the balloon.

Now the weight of the balloon and air is less than the thrust of the surrounding air. The surrounding air rushes in under the balloon, pushing it upwards. So the balloon flies.

The balloon comes down again when the air inside cools, allowing the air outside to rush in and fill the balloon. This makes the balloon heavier and it falls back to earth.

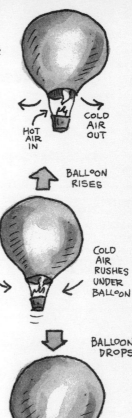

HOT AIR IN

COLD AIR OUT

BALLOON RISES

COLD AIR RUSHES UNDER BALLOON

BALLOON DROPS

FIRE GOES OUT, COLD AIR RUSHES IN

A small step for sheep, a large quack for duck-kind

On September 16, 1783, a huge crowd gathered at the Royal Palace at Versailles. The king and queen of France and all the people of their court watched the Montgolfier brothers prepare their hot-air balloon for its historic big day out.

You have to remember that balloons were high-tech in 1783.[4] So the crowd was very excited, just the way we might feel if we were watching a Mars landing craft.

And what a beauty this new balloon was. Made from varnished cloth, it was 19 meters (62 feet) high and 12 meters (39 feet) across. That's about as high as a six-story apartment building and as wide as a garbage truck.[5]

Étienne filled the balloon's brazier[6] with wood and straw and old boots. He struck a match and lit the fuel. The blazing fire gave off clouds of black smoke and plenty of hot air. The balloon filled in only seven minutes. Sixteen men were struggling to hold it down. At Étienne's signal they let go.

[4] This was the same year that the American Revolution ended, which was fought on foot or horseback, not from the cockpit of a fighter jet!

[5] Or as high as 10 refrigerators and as wide as 16 armadillos.

[6] A brazier is not a piece of ladies' underclothing. That just wouldn't work. A brazier is a metal can that can safely hold a fire. The balloonist kept feeding it with straw and wood and other stuff and that's where the hot air came from. But it wasn't all that safe. Lots of sparks would fly off the fire and often the balloon caught fire. The pilots would try to put out the spot fires with wet sponges on long sticks.

Everybody gasped in amazement as the brilliantly painted balloon rose quickly into the sky. And the passengers looked down at their amazing bird's-eye view of the Earth below.

Did I say bird's-eye view? Let me remind you that this wonderful occasion could have been the . . .

. . . first ever manned balloon flight.

But the Montgolfier brothers didn't choose a man, or a woman, to pilot this first flight. Not a girl or a boy, either. Étienne wanted the first pilot to be a sheep. Joseph favored a cow.

I would have voted for an elephant. That would have been really spectacular!

But the Montgolfiers were most likely worried about choosing a human pilot, just in case something went wrong. Killing a pilot on the first public hot-air balloon flight might result in bad publicity. A lot of bad publicity!!

So the brothers decided the pilot should be a sheep. And to stop the sheep getting lonely they teamed him with a duck. Naturally! And to keep the sheep and duck in line they sent a rooster along, too. Why not? I suppose if the balloon flight were to end in death and disaster, at least they could cut their losses and eat the crew!

The flight was a great success and ensured the future of ballooning. Unfortunately we have no video record of this event,[7] but I imagine it might have gone a bit like this.

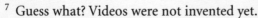

7 Guess what? Videos were not invented yet.

Get 'em while they're hot!

On November 21, 1783, two months and five days after this first heroic flight of the sheep, duck and rooster, a big crowd arrived at a royal palace west of Paris, in the Bois de Boulogne.

Today, it is hard to believe how exciting this hot-air balloon idea was. But in France everyone was talking about balloons as the next big thing.[8]

This time, Joseph and Étienne Montgolfier planned a public manned flight. With real humans!

To pilot instead of the sheep, the brothers selected François Pilâtre de Rozier. Filling in for the rooster was François d'Arlandes.[9]

De Rozier was a real balloon nut who desperately wanted to be the first man to fly. He was also a friend of the king, so the Montgolfiers weren't going to say no to him. They needed the king's support.

---

[8] Like hula-hoops today . . . I mean, yesterday.
[9] The duck wanted to go along as navigator, but someone ate her.

The other pilot, d'Arlandes, was a bit of a rich fool and a good friend of Joseph Montgolfier. The brothers had long ago promised him he could be on the first flight. In exchange he probably helped them out with some much-needed spare cash. Ballooning was an expensive hobby.

At the appointed time, de Rozier and d'Arlandes climbed aboard the Montgolfiers' huge balloon, which was brilliantly decorated in the king's colors. The balloon was a whopping 23 meters (75 feet) high and 15 meters (49 feet) in diameter, with a wicker basket 5 meters (16 feet) wide hanging underneath. It was fueled by a straw-fed fire in a brazier hanging under a hole in the bottom of the balloon.

The pilots fed the fire, the balloon filled with hot air, and when the attendants could no longer hold the balloon down, they cut the ropes and up it went.

For the first time in human history, people were flying.

Imagine the excitement of de Rozier and d'Arlandes with their bird's-eye view of Paris. In fact, d'Arlandes was so carried away looking at the view that

he kept forgetting to stoke the balloon's fire. Four or five times the fire died down and the balloon dropped dangerously close to the ground. The balloon caught fire a few times, too, but they put the fires out with a wet sponge on a long stick.

At one point the seam started to tear apart and they had a near-collision with a windmill, but de Rozier stayed cool. Somehow they managed to keep aloft for about 25 minutes and traveled about 4 kilometers (2½ miles). When they eventually ran out of fuel, the balloon dropped slowly down and landed safely in a field.

And so ended the first ever manned balloon flight.

Let's find a more dangerous way to fly!

The next big challenge for balloonists was to cross the English Channel, a 26-kilometer-wide (16-mile-wide) body of water between England and France.[10]

[10] I wonder if the French people call it the French Channel?

In the 1780s a hot-air balloon couldn't possibly carry enough fuel to travel that distance. Modern balloons use gas cylinders for fuel, but in 1780 gas cylinders hadn't been invented.

Some balloonists experimented with hydrogen gas instead of hot air. Because hydrogen is the lightest gas, it floats above air. The drawback is that hydrogen is very dangerous. It explodes really well and easily and very often. It only takes the tiniest spark and . . .

KKKKAAAAAABBBOOOOMMMM!!!

So flying around in a hydrogen balloon was a bit like flying around in a plane made entirely of dynamite.

There were other problems, too. Because hydrogen is so light, some of the first balloons floated up very high very quickly. At great altitudes the air is freezing cold. Some balloons eventually returned to earth with their crew still sitting in the basket, frozen to death.

At high altitudes the atmosphere is also much thinner, so the pilots were often left with no air to breathe. Or the hydrogen gas in the balloon expanded so much that the balloon eventually burst. So, if the pilots didn't freeze or choke to death, their balloon would blow up and they would plunge back to earth.

And parachutes hadn't been invented yet, either.

A wee problem of ballast

To begin with, hydrogen balloons exploded only occasionally, so people were not afraid to experiment with them. Two balloonists, Jean-Pierre Blanchard and John Jeffries, accepted the challenge of flying across the English Channel. They believed that only a hydrogen balloon could stay aloft that distance. For several months, they waited in Dover, England, for just the right wind conditions. Their balloon was a weird-looking thing.

On January 7, 1785 the weather was perfect. Blanchard and Jeffries took off and their balloon sailed majestically over the English Channel. They opened a bottle of bubbly and began to relax.

Suddenly Blanchard realized their balloon was rising too high, too quickly. Not good if it flew too high . . . well, you know about that.

HYDROGEN-FILLED BALLOON

GONDOLA WITH SILK-COVERED PADDLES, A RUDDER AND A CRANKABLE PROPELLER

BLANCHARD AND JEFFRIES CELEBRATE WITH CHAMPAGNE.

UP
DOWN

GASP! BRRR! POP! PLUNGE!

Blanchard pulled on a rope and released some of the hydrogen gas through a valve at the top of the balloon. The balloon began to descend, and the pilots returned to their bubbly. But Blanchard had released too much gas and now the balloon dropped dangerously low.

If a hot-air balloon drops too low, all the pilot needs to do is throw more fuel on the fire. But that's not a good idea in a hydrogen balloon. Light a match and you're barbecued.

Instead Blanchard and Jeffries carried ballast, usually sandbags. When their balloon dropped too low, they simply threw out some ballast and their balloon would rise up again.

As they floated across the English Channel, Blanchard realized that his balloon was slowly leaking hydrogen. Rather than crash into the sea, they kept throwing out ballast. When they ran out of ballast, they started pulling apart the gondola and throwing that into the sea. Two and a half hours later, most of that was gone, too. So was everything else they could lay their hands on, including most of their clothing.

SSSSS.....

BLANCHARD UNDIES

GONDOLA STRIPPED BARE

BLANCHARD AND JEFFRIES STRIPPED BARE

And in one last mighty effort to avoid smashing into the cliffs of Calais in France, Blanchard and Jeffries urinated into the sea.[11]

[11] If this didn't work, they probably would have sawed their own arms off.

Weird, I know.[12] But urinating must have released powerful forces. Luckily for the boys, just as they were about to crash into the Calais cliffs, a wind sprang up and blew them over to safety.

Blanchard and Jeffries had amazed the world by conquering the English Channel in a balloon. And this feat now excited other inventors and adventurers to look for even greater challenges.

Hot-air hydrogen sandwich to go

Before we leave ballooning, let us return to François Pilâtre de Rozier. Remember him? He was one of the pilots on the Montgolfiers' first manned flight in 1783. When he heard about Jeffries and Blanchard's flight across the English Channel, de Rozier was very jealous. He had been planning a similar flight and was now forced to rethink.

He realized that controlling a hydrogen balloon was very difficult. If the balloon flew too high,

[12] Except they'd thrown their saw overboard.

the pilot used a valve to let gas out and if it flew too low, he could throw out ballast. But there was no way of making more hydrogen gas during a flight.

Hot-air balloons were more controllable. The pilot could simply stoke up the fire to rise higher and let the fire die down to drop lower. The big problem with a hot-air balloon was carrying enough fuel to allow you to travel a long distance, like the 26-kilometer (16-mile) English Channel.

De Rozier designed a new sandwich balloon, which combined the best features of both. Attached to the gondola was a hot-air balloon, and sitting above that was a hydrogen balloon. The power of the two balloons would be enough to lift the gondola up. Then the pilots could use the fire of the hot-air balloon to maintain that height. When the fuel ran out, they could continue flying with the hydrogen balloon. With luck, they wouldn't run out of ballast or gas.

There was just one small problem. I can see it. I think you can see it. I don't know why de Rozier didn't see it. A hot-air balloon, driven by fire, sitting directly below a balloon filled with the most explosive gas in the universe ... What was de Rozier thinking? Either he never thought it would be dangerous, or he just thought, "No problem. It'll be just *fine*."

But it wasn't!

De Rozier planned to fly east to west from France to England, against the usual west-to-east wind. This was the reverse of the way Jeffries and Blanchard had flown. De Rozier and his assistant Pierre Romain sat around in France for many months waiting for an east-west wind.

Eventually it came. Early one morning, they lifted off and were soon flying high on their way to England. But they didn't get very far. It is hard to know exactly what happened, but probably some sparks from the brazier landed on the hydrogen balloon, which exploded with a BIG BANG!!

Even if it survived the blast, the hot-air balloon wouldn't have been large enough to keep the gondola aloft. So it plummeted to earth, killing both de Rozier and Romain. This was the first recorded air disaster. De Rozier, the first-ever aviator, was dead.

STUPID BALLOONS!

Ballooning didn't die with him. More than two centuries later, pilots fly around the globe in balloons filled with very safe helium gas. And if things do go wrong, they have a special device to help them—the parachute! It was invented in 1797 by André-Jacques Garnerin and quickly became the pilot's best friend.

Balloonists became frustrated at being able to go only where the wind took them. They dreamed of a form of powered flight that would let them fly whenever and wherever they wanted. It was obvious balloons could never do that. It would take more than 100 years before this dream would be realized.

Chapter 4

That wing thing

Fixed wings

Once inventors accepted that lighter-than-air balloons could never deliver the dream of controlled and powered flight, they switched their thinking to heavier-than-air craft. They produced many fantastic designs for airplanes, some looking like sailing ships with huge wings, rudders and oars paddling through the sky. But these were impractical, and the world was still waiting for one sensible scientific model of the future airplane.

Then along came George Cayley, a wealthy nobleman from Yorkshire, England. While still just a teenager he built a working model helicopter, explored basic kite shapes and even built and tested models of fixed-wing airplanes.

But George's truly great breakthrough came in 1799, when he drew a simple sketch of his vision of what a plane might look like. Amazingly he predicted the layout of every plane from the simplest ultra-light to the grandest Jumbo 747. Cayley's imagined airplane could not possibly fly, but that wasn't important. He had succeeded in changing forever the thinking on aircraft design.

He had accepted that imitating birds with flapping wings simply wouldn't work. Instead his sketch showed a plane whose engine was separate from its body and wings. It seems obvious today, but at the time it was a radical idea.

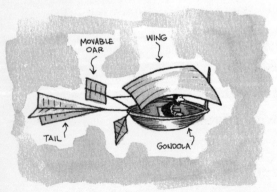

George adds, Sarah multiplies

George Cayley married his childhood sweetheart Sarah Walker in 1795. They shared an interest in mathematics and aviation and in 1804 they started building gliders together. Their first model looked a bit like a kite on a spear. Unfortunately it was a complete failure! When launched, it immediately dived, crashed and broke up.

Did they give up? Yes. They took up gardening instead.

Actually I lied about that. They were so *obsessed* with fixed-wing gliders that there was no way they were going to give up. Instead they redesigned their glider, attaching vertical and horizontal tails. It still didn't fly much better, so they pulled it apart again and rebuilt it entirely.

Their next model had wings with an upward vee, and a tail with a downward vee. Because the vees balanced each other out, this glider proved to be very stable in flight.

George and Sarah had just invented and flown the first ever working model glider. The year was 1809.

This upward vee is called a dihedral wing. It is the shape all modern plane wings have. Take a look at a passenger jet and you will see that its wings slope upwards towards the outside, preventing the plane rolling from side to side.

BIRD WINGS HAVE A NATURAL 'VEE' OR DIHEDRAL SHAPE

George and Sarah also worked out that for greatest stability the wings should be at the center of gravity of the plane, where its weight balances. They also added movable flaps to the wings to steer the glider up or down.

CAYLEY DESIGNED HIS GLIDERS WITH THIS DIHEDRAL SHAPE

At some point Sarah became too busy caring for the family, leaving George to continue with his experiments alone. Exploring powered flight, he discovered that engines would

THE WING IS PLACED AT THE CENTER OF GRAVITY

need their maximum power at take-off. Keeping the plane in the air would require less power.

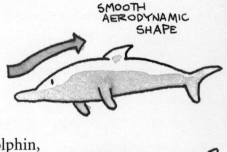

SMOOTH
AERODYNAMIC
SHAPE

He also experimented with shapes that would give less drag through the air. He discovered the best shape was that of a dolphin, which is roughly the shape of most modern planes.

A ten-year-old hero, and a flying coachman

George Cayley continued his experiments with gliders and in 1849 he built his biggest and best so far. This model glider featured a triple-decker wing, and was called a triplane. It also had a gondola hanging underneath and several cross-shaped tails. This model performed brilliantly in many test flights. But George was desperate to see how it would fly with a live pilot.

Now if he was one of the ballooning Montgolfier
brothers he would have given the pilot's job to a duck
or a sheep. But George wanted a real live human pilot.
This model glider, while almost full-sized, could not
support an adult pilot so George needed to find a
smaller-scale pilot.

A local ten-year-old boy walked by the Cayley
house at just the wrong time. George decided he was
the perfect size and showed him over the model glider

and somehow managed to convince him to be its pilot. Unfortunately we know nothing about the boy. But what ten-year-old child wouldn't jump at the chance to fly in a model glider?

George Cayley sat the boy in the gondola, and without giving him time to change his mind, ran ahead dragging the glider behind on a rope. It quickly lifted up in the air, a bit like a kite. And with George towing the glider against the breeze, the boy hung on nervously. He flew a short distance across the field before lightly touching down on the grass. This was a momentous event in the history of flight. And this lucky kid now had some story to tell his grandchildren. "I was the first person ever to fly in a fixed-wing aircraft. And I was only ten years old!"[1]

After this success, Cayley was unstoppable.

---

[1]   I bet he would have forgotten to mention that the glider was attached to a rope.

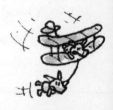

In 1853, even though he was 80 years old, he built his first full-sized glider. This time, he gave the honor of being pilot to his coachman. It was an honor his coachman didn't really want. But once again George managed to convince him.

Cayley pushed the glider and pilot off a hill on his farm. They flew flat and low for a distance of 500 meters ($^1/_3$ mile) across a small valley and crash-landed on the other side. Cayley's coachman had become the first person to fly freely in a winged aircraft. This was yet another great moment in aviation history. But the coachman was not celebrating. While his flight had been smooth, his landing was a bit rough—violent, even! He wasn't badly injured, but he'd had enough of being pushed off hills in a glider. He declared his career as a pilot was over. In fact, he resigned as Cayley's coachman as well, and was last seen running back to town.

Meanwhile old George had a grin from one 80-year-old ear to the other. Not only had his piloted glider just flown a record distance, but he had shown the world that fixed-wing aircraft were the way of the future.

48

That magical lift

Did you know there are Laws of Gas Behavior? They're like school rules for gases. Well, I didn't know this. I thought gases could do what they liked. I know I have produced a few lawless gases in my time. Haven't we all?

In 1738, Daniel Bernoulli discovered an important law of gas behavior. It was to prove very useful to the future of airplane wing design, but nobody realized at the time. This law states: if you increase the speed of a gas, you lower its pressure.

Now that doesn't mean much to me, but it meant a lot to an Englishman called Horatio Phillips. He was yet another person obsessed with flight and, at the time, was trying to design better wings. In 1884, he succeeded in inventing the curved airfoil wing shape.

Using Bernoulli's Gas Law, Horatio was able to explain why this wing shape worked better than any other. It goes something like this. As this wing moves through the sky it cuts through the air, which passes above and below the wing.

The air that passes above has to travel a greater distance than the air that passes below. That is because the wing has a curved upper surface. So that air has to move faster. And because it moves faster, its air pressure is lower.[2] In the same way, the air below the wing moves slower, so its air pressure becomes greater.

Lower air pressure above the wing and greater air pressure below the wing! That means the wing is sucked from above and pushed from below. So the wing rises up, taking the plane with it. This is called lift. And it is this lift that makes every winged airplane fly.

We have no record of Horatio Phillips ever building and testing wings, but he certainly wrote many papers about them, which other aviation inventors read.

TAKE A THIN STRIP OF PAPER.

BLOW ACROSS THE TOP OF THE PAPER.

THE LOWER AIR PRESSURE ABOVE THE PAPER, AND THE GREATER PRESSURE BELOW, MAKES THE PAPER RISE.

LOWER PRESSURE

AIRFLOW

GREATER PRESSURE

[2] That's because of that Law of Gas Behavior I was telling you about.

50

From 1884 onwards they started building their gliders and planes with Horatio Phillips's airfoil wings.

The Aerial Steam Carriage

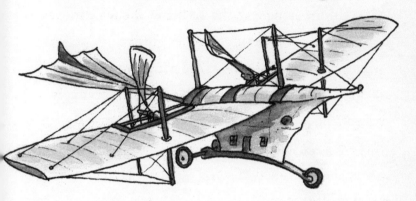

About 40 years before Phillips's amazing discovery, in 1843, two Englishmen, William Henson and John Stringfellow, were designing self-powered gliders. They had built a large-scale model called the Aerial Steam Carriage.

It featured upward-sweeping wings (dihedral), a separate tail with rudders and elevators, and twin propellers driven by a lightweight steam engine.[3]

[3] As lightweight as was possible at the time, which was not very lightweight!

CRASH!

It looked great, but sadly it would never fly. Its small steam engine just wasn't powerful enough to lift it off the ground.

But the Aerial Steam Carriage did inspire others. In 1890, a French engineer, Clément Ader, built a model glider called *Eole*. Its steam engine developed just enough power for *Eole* to take off and fly for over 50 meters (164 feet) at the frightening height of 20 centimeters (8 inches).[4] Not very spectacular, maybe, but it was probably the first successful powered flight.

Six years later, an American called Samuel Langley built a twin-winged, steam-powered model plane called *Aerodrome*. It was much more stable in the air than Ader's *Eole* and managed to fly the spectacular distance of over one kilometer (just over ¹/₂ mile).

It took Langley seven more years to build a full-sized version of *Aerodrome*, but sadly this kept crashing on take-off, leaving Langley frustrated and dispirited. While Langley understood a great deal about the science of wings, tails and rudders, he knew almost

[4]   That's about the height of this book.

nothing about the art of controlling a glider in the air.

Aviation would never take the final step to controlled and powered flight until brave inventors started risking their lives in the sky to learn the basic techniques of controlling a glider in flight. And probably the most daring of all these inventors was a man called Otto Lilienthal.

The world's first aviator was a Pomeranian!

It's true Otto Lilienthal, the world's first aviator, was a Pomeranian. But while some dogs are Pomeranians, not all Pomeranians are dogs. In fact, Otto was human. He was born in 1848 in a place called Pomerania, in the old Kingdom of Prussia. It is now a part of modern Germany, but back then it was a separate country.

As a child, Otto was always fascinated by birds. So you won't be surprised to learn that as an adult, Otto became obsessed with flight. During the daytime, he made his living running a small engineering factory, but at night Otto would design ornithopters.

He soon realized these crazy contraptions could never fly, so he switched to building fixed-wing gliders. Otto would run around his big property dragging his gliders behind on a string, desperately trying to get them to fly. Then someone told him that George Cayley had built his own hill to launch his gliders from. Well, of course Otto Lilienthal immediately wanted a hill as well. In 1891, he scavenged some dirt from a nearby construction site and built himself a hill 18 meters (60 feet) high. Now he could fly his gliders whichever way the wind blew.

Otto's gliders looked a lot like modern hang-gliders. His most successful one, number 11 of 1894, featured huge wings spanning 4 meters (13 feet), and a tail very like the tails on modern planes.

Lilienthal believed that aviation would never progress until pilots learned how to control their gliders in flight. And the only way to do this was through trial and error. This is what sets Otto Lilienthal apart from other aviators of the time. He was not only an inventor, but also a daredevil pilot willing to risk his life for science.

Lilienthal sat in
a harness under the wings
and practiced controlling the
balance of his glider by shifting his weight around.

Can't you just imagine him jumping off that hill?
Getting the feel of the wind. Leaning to one side and
smiling as his glider flew around in a slow arc. Probably
singing a little song as he looked at the world below
him. Then leaning back to tilt his wings slightly upward
and allow his glider to glide to a gentle landing.

Otto Lilienthal flew this particular glider over 2500 times, regularly covering distances of 200–300 meters (650–1000 feet). He worked very scientifically, making notes about each test flight. He recorded distances and wind conditions and noted each adjustment he had made to the glider and its controls. With all this practice, Otto Lilienthal naturally became an expert aviator.

At one point, he even tried adding a light steam engine to his craft, and came very close to being the first to achieve controlled and powered flight. He might well have succeeded but for a tragic accident.

One day in 1896, he was flying over a field when a sudden gust of wind caught his glider, which stalled and crashed to the ground. Otto Lilienthal was badly injured and died the next day.

Because he had been such a dedicated scientist, Otto Lilienthal's notes and sketches ensured that what he had discovered through his experiments would be passed on to future aviation inventors. But it was also his bravery and daring as a test pilot that inspired so many future aviators. They spoke of Otto Lilienthal as the "world's first true aviator."

Chapter 5

Up, up and away

Powered flight

After Otto Lilienthal's death, the race was truly on
to develop the world's first true airplane. There were
two main contenders, Samuel Langley[1] and Orville
and Wilbur Wright.[2]

Samuel Langley had built a huge catapult on his
houseboat on the Potamac River in Virginia. He used
to fling his latest inventions off it to see how they flew.
Usually they didn't.

[1] Remember him?—he was the inventor of the spectacularly
unsuccessful *Aerodrome* in the last chapter.
[2] Actually, that's three contenders!

Langley had been building model planes for years, starting off with tiny propeller-driven planes powered by rubber bands. He made many mistakes and happily smashed up hundreds of models, but each time he learned something. That's trial and error again!

When he finally did succeed in building a model glider that would fly, he tried adding a steam engine. But his engines were always much too heavy and his planes flew like pianos.[3]

So Langley went back to the drawing board and came up with a new design. It had two sets of wings, spanning 4.5 meters (15 feet), set one behind the other. He built two of these planes, *Aerodrome #5* and *#6*.

In 1896 he catapulted *Aerodrome #6* off his houseboat, but it broke up on take-off.

---

[3] Have you ever seen a piano fly? Actually, they plummet.

Not one to give up easily, Langley immediately launched *Aerodrome #5*. It managed to stay in the air, flying into a light breeze, driven by its tiny one-horsepower steam engine. Weighing only 15 kilograms (33 pounds), this engine was about the weight of a medium-sized dog, but probably not as powerful.

Aerodrome #5 rose up about 30 meters (100 feet) and flew in large circles for 90 seconds, covering around 800 meters ($^1/_2$ mile). And when it finally ran out of steam, it gently plopped back down into the river.

Langley celebrated by fishing it out of the water, drying it off and flying it again. Same result!

Excited by this success, Langley rushed back home to repair and improve both *Aerodrome*s. Six months later he returned to the Potamac River and this time *Aerodrome #6* flew in even larger circles for a new record of 105 seconds.

Langley had truly achieved powered flight, but he still had no way of controlling his plane. Basically it flew where it wanted to. Langley needed an airplane big enough to carry a pilot, and that would require a much more powerful engine.

After many trials on improved engine designs, Langley finally realized that a steam engine powerful enough to launch a plane was always going to be too heavy. There had to be another way.

The Wright engine

Samuel Langley was not aware that, not that far away, someone was close to solving this engine problem.

Two brothers, Wilbur and Orville Wright, ran a bicycle factory in Dayton, Ohio, and were naturals at playing with machines. They had constructed their own factory, machines, tools and bike parts. And eventually, when they had sold enough bicycles to make themselves rich, they devoted their spare time to their favorite hobby—experimenting with airplanes. They had read everything about aviation they could lay their hands on, and had built many gliders inspired by the experiments of Lilienthal and Cayley and by Langley's 1896 flights.

Best of all, the Wrights had designed and built a simple, single-cylinder gas engine to power their bike-building machines. They realized this engine could be used to power their airplanes. That would leave only one more obstacle to them developing the first airplane—controlling the plane in flight.

To solve that problem, the Wrights returned to what they knew best, bikes. When you need to turn on a bike, you lean to one side and Bob's your uncle, around you go.[4] The Wrights thought this might work just as well with planes.

Wilbur Wright had observed eagles flying around his home. He saw that they turned by simply lifting up the feathers on the end of one wing and dropping down those on the opposite wing. So he devised a method of twisting the wings of his gliders to create similar banked turns.

In 1900, the brothers built a glider with a wingspan of 5.5 meters (18 feet) and took it to a windy place called Kitty Hawk, which had sand dunes perfect for test flights. Their wing-twisting method gave them great control in flight, but now

---

[4] Yes, Bob is still your uncle!

their wings weren't giving
enough lift. The brothers
returned home determined
to solve this new problem.

A year later, they returned to
Kitty Hawk with a
new improved
wing, spanning
7 meters
(23 feet).
They had also
added a smaller
horizontal wing
forward of the main
wing, which gave this glider
much more stability.

But this improved wing still couldn't
provide enough lift and the wing-twisting method
was proving to be unreliable. Dangerous, in fact!

The Wrights realized that the shape of their wing
cross-section, based on Lilienthal's earlier designs,

wasn't going to work. They
returned home again and
built and tested over 200 new
cross-sections. Imagine
the work involved in that!
They made the wings
longer and thinner, which
seemed to create enough lift
and less drag.

After a few
more test
flights at
Kitty Hawk,
Orville
added a
movable rear
tail rudder. This gave
the brothers the stability they
had been searching for. Now they had
a fully controllable glider, and after more tests they
bettered the world record for controlled flight.

The man who walked on water . . . almost!

About the same time the Wrights were conducting their test flights in Ohio, an Australian engineer called Lawrence Hargrave was close to building his own successful powered airplane.

His mind played with all sorts of strange inventions, the weirdest of which was his special walk-on-water boots. Okay, they didn't work, but what a great idea!

Hargrave was rich and lived on a big estate just outside of Sydney. Because he didn't have to work for a living, he spent his time studying how birds flew and making model ornithopters.

In 1884 he made one powered by a rubber band, which actually flew several meters (15–20 feet). Excited, he built a bigger 16-rubber-band model, which flew over 33 meters (108 feet). Driven by that success, Hargrave then built an even bigger ornithopter with a handle for the pilot to crank to move the wings. Unfortunately, it didn't fly at all!

Hargrave decided that his ornithopter needed an engine. So he designed and built a single-cylinder gas engine, which worked very well but lacked power. Now Hargrave immersed himself in engine design, building another 35 engines, including the first reliable rotary engine.[5] He also designed the first jet engines, but could never get them to work properly.

Eventually Hargrave gave up on ornithopters and started designing model fixed-wing gliders, still powered by rubber bands. In 1889, his best design flew 34 meters (112 feet). In 1891, he built a larger model plane with a rotary engine and propeller. It stayed aloft for 8 seconds and flew 40 meters (131 feet). Although Hargrave redesigned this plane many times, he never managed to get it to fly any farther.

What Hargrave never discovered was that his propellers were set at the wrong angle to deliver all the engine's power. If he had managed to solve this problem, he might well have been the first man to fly. But the world of invention is full of "if only's."

[5]   Which are still used in planes today.

Hargrave became so frustrated with fixed-wing aircraft that he returned to ornithopters. Bad career move!

Always curious, in 1893 Hargrave took to flying kites. He invented the box kite and at one point he linked four of them together and lifted himself up 5 meters (16 feet). These experiments with kites led Hargrave to discover the correct airfoil wing shape. Excited by his wing discovery, Hargrave began to experiment with gliders again. He developed a deep parabolic wing with a thick leading edge, which gave enormous lift. This was the same wing shape the Wright brothers had discovered in their experiments.

Engines and propellers

By 1902, the Wrights led the world in glider design. While they had overcome many of the problems of controlling flight, they still needed a stronger, lighter engine and a better propeller.

In 1903, they built their own wind tunnel and began testing their various propeller designs. Eventually they developed a propeller that delivered maximum power. It was a twisted airfoil shape and is still used on planes today.

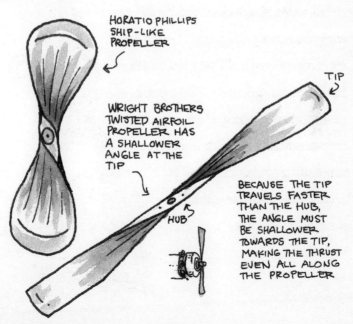

HORATIO PHILLIPS SHIP-LIKE PROPELLER

WRIGHT BROTHERS TWISTED AIRFOIL PROPELLER HAS A SHALLOWER ANGLE AT THE TIP

TIP

BECAUSE THE TIP TRAVELS FASTER THAN THE HUB, THE ANGLE MUST BE SHALLOWER TOWARDS THE TIP, MAKING THE THRUST EVEN ALL ALONG THE PROPELLER

HUB

Meanwhile, all over the world, inventors were trying to design a powerful lightweight gas engine. Samuel Langley and his head engineer, Charles Manly, built a 100-kilogram (220-pound), five-cylinder rotary engine. This was a beauty and much better than the engines the Wrights had. But the Wrights' propellers were better than Langley's. If only they had shared their ideas. Together they could have achieved great things!! But they were now rivals in a race to achieve powered and controlled flight. Cooperation was never going to happen.

The Wrights hoped they might be able to use car engines, but these proved much too heavy for aircraft. So they returned to doing what they had always done. They developed their own 90-kilogram (200-pound), 12-horsepower cast-aluminum gas engine.

They attached this engine to the lower wing of their latest glider, connecting it by chains to two propellers. The whole plane weighed 340 kilograms (750 pounds) and had a 13-meter (43-foot) wingspan, giving about 51 square meters (170 square feet) of wing area.[6]

[6] That's about half the area of the average school classroom.

They returned to Kitty Hawk in February 1903, aware that their rival, Samuel Langley, was close to success. In early trials their new engine blew up, and the Wrights had to rush back home to Dayton to cast a new one.

Up, up, up . . . down!

Meanwhile back on his houseboat on the Potamac, Langley and Manly prepared their new airplane, *Aerodrome A*, for its first flight. This model had a larger wing area than the Wrights' plane and a more powerful engine.

Launching from the catapult was a great advantage. It meant they didn't need as powerful an engine as the Wrights. On October 7, 1903, *Aerodrome A* shot into the air, flew briefly and almost immediately crashed into the river. Luckily Manly swam clear, but *Aerodrome A* was totally wrecked. They managed to salvage the engine and bits of the frame and returned home to rebuild it, but it would be December before they were ready for another try.

Manly had flown only a few times and really didn't know how to control his plane. The problem with their catapulting take-offs was that the plane would either fly or crash! Manly couldn't do short test flights like the Wrights were able to do.[7] But they didn't think this mattered, because they believed their plane was so stable in the air. That's confidence!

The Wrights were launching their planes from the ground, which enabled them to do hundreds of very short, low test flights. They could run alongside adjusting their plane as it flew, developing a great feel for how to control their planes, just as Lilienthal had done.

When Langley and Manly did return in December to fly the rebuilt *Aerodrome A*, it flew off the catapult, flipped over on its back, broke into pieces and sank into the river. Manly was nearly knocked unconscious, almost drowned and came close to freezing to death.[8]

[7] If the plane crashed, you had to haul it out of the river, dry it off and try again. Not an easy process.
[8] Why was Langley doing test flights in an icy river in the middle of winter?

70

While Manly survived, Langley's project didn't. Humiliated, he returned to his museum job in Washington and gave up aviation altogether.

Yes, we have take-off!

Meanwhile, back in Kitty Hawk in October 1903, the Wrights were not aware that their rival, Langley, would soon withdraw from the race. They had resumed flights with a completely new plane, the *Wright Flyer*, but were being constantly frustrated by a series of equipment failures.

Finally on December 14, 1903, with Wilbur at the controls, the *Wright Flyer* slipped down its specially made wooden track and lifted into the air. It flew at a height of about 5 meters (16 feet), covering 20 meters (66 feet) before it jagged upwards, stalled and crashed back to Earth. Fortunately, neither plane nor Wilbur was too badly damaged.

On December 17, 1903, it was Orville's turn. He lay down on the lower wing and gripped the controls.

He held tight the brake-rope. The engine roared, Orville let go of the rope and the *Flyer* raced down the track.

It was airborne before it reached the end, rising 5 meters (16 feet) into the air. Doing a wild 10 kilometers (6 miles) per hour,[9] it flew for about 40 meters (130 feet) before lightly touching down again.

Small though those numbers might be, they were historic. This was truly sustained, powered and controlled flight.

But how controlled was it? Orville believed that during the entire flight of 12 seconds, he was not really ever in control of the plane. He was still just going along for the ride.

[9]   That's about a medium running pace.

For the rest of that day Wilbur and Orville took turns, each time flying greater distances but never really feeling they had the *Flyer* under their control.

On the fourth attempt Wilbur managed to steer the *Flyer* along the beach for a mammoth 59 seconds. He covered 280 meters (918 feet) before the wobbles got too much and he had to set it down.

Orville rushed up and embraced his brother.

This time they really had
become the first people to achieve
powered and controlled flight.

After December 17, 1903, the world would never
be the same.

Nor would the *Wright Flyer*! In the middle of their
big celebrations, a sudden strong wind blew up, lifting
the *Flyer* off the ground and tumbling it down the
beach. Wings broke, wood splintered, wires snapped,
the engine was torn off and the *Flyer* was destroyed.

It really didn't matter, because the Wright brothers
had realized their dream. No other inventors anywhere
in the world were even close to matching the Wrights'
designs for wings, propellers, controls and engine.
It would take them years to catch up.

Did Wilbur and Orville hold a press conference
to tell the world the big news?

No, that was not the Wright way. They just sent
a telegram to let their family know of their success,
packed up and went home for Christmas. When
reporters came to visit, the brothers simply admitted
they had flown, but refused to give any details.

The Wright brothers quietly patented all their inventions, especially the wing-twisting idea. They believed that because they had done the hard scientific work, they should be allowed to profit from it. Fair enough, I suppose. But if Lilienthal, Cayley and others had refused to share *their* discoveries, the Wrights might never have achieved their success.

During 1904 and 1905 the Wright brothers held many more successful flights in a rebuilt *Flyer*, constantly improving the plane's handling and finally overcoming its instability. On October 5, 1905, Wilbur flew around their paddock 30 times, covering a distance of 38 kilometers (24 miles) in 39 minutes.

The Wright brothers went on to be the first great aviation entrepreneurs, setting up the Wright Company, which sold thousands of planes around the world. When Wilbur died of typhoid fever in 1912, Orville took over the running of the company and eventually retired a very wealthy man. He died in 1948.

Across that Channel again

I cannot finish without telling you about the Great Cross-Channel Challenge. Lord Northcliffe, who owned the London *Daily Mail* newspaper, offered a prize of £1000 to the first person to cross the English Channel in a plane. Three teams set themselves for the challenge.

One was a Frenchman called Hubert Latham.
Most people thought he would win because he was
the best organized. Another contender was Count
Charles de Lambert of Russia, who used his wealth to
buy two *Wright Flyers*.

The third contestant was Louis Blériot, flying in
a borrowed plane, using borrowed money.
No one expected him to win. His plane was the
smallest and the least tested, and the engine was
not considered powerful enough to carry
him across the Channel.

If you think that was enough to
count him out, let me tell you more.
He was uncoordinated, he had one leg
in plaster, he followed his instincts too much
and he was a lousy pilot.[10]

Guess what? He won.

The Russian count crashed both his planes in
practice, and never even made it to the starting line.
This left Latham and Blériot sitting in Calais, France,

[10] And his mom probably didn't love him, either.

waiting for the right weather. When it finally arrived on July 25, 1909, Blériot woke before dawn, stuck his crutches in his plane and took off across the Channel.

This was an all-or-nothing flight for Blériot. If he crashed, he would be financially ruined. And probably dead! If he succeeded, he might just be able to restore his fortune. Maybe that was the incentive Blériot needed, because he doggedly flew on towards England despite the cold, his aching leg and the lack of a compass to guide him. He had no idea of the weather he was flying into. He wasn't even sure if his engine would be strong enough to lift him over the cliffs of Dover at the other end.

Blériot became lost, but was resourceful enough to follow ships into Dover harbor. After a spectacular crash landing in a field, Blériot was rushed to London, where he was given a hero's welcome and the precious £1000.

Blériot used his prize money to set up an aircraft factory. During World War I he built and sold more than 10 000 planes to the Allied forces, which earned him a great fortune. He died a wealthy man.

And then . . .

From this point, the history of flight goes a bit
like this.

Better and bigger planes are built, in wartime guns
are stuck on them and bombs dropped from them
and many planes crash, so better engines are built
and planes fly faster with parachutes for the pilot and
they fly around the world with more passengers and
more powerful engines, two engines, four engines,
then six and, sadly, bigger plane disasters and then
turbo engines and better guns and bigger bombs
and, KABLAMM!! jet engines fly faster higher and
really, really big planes with hundreds of passengers,
really big plane disasters and black box recorders and
broken sound barriers and jumbo jets like big, heavy,
cumbersome flying pigs and war planes with more
guns and bigger bombs and cluster bombs and nuclear
bombs and radar-avoiding stealth bombers and rockets
flying to the moon and Mars and Jupiter and Pluto and
beyond to the stars.

Which leaves one
question unanswered:
is it true that pigs fly?
Well, it just so happens
that one did once.

In America, a passenger convinced an airline
that his "therapeutic companion pet" needed to fly
with him, first class. The stewards were expecting
a guide dog, but what arrived instead was a pig.
Eventually 200 passengers and one pig took off from
Philadelphia airport.

Close to landing, the pig got scared and confused
and started running up and down the aisles, banging
on the cockpit door and upsetting the other passengers.
Perhaps they were serving ham!

"It will never happen again," the embarrassed
airline crew apologized.

But at least now you know, it's true, pigs
do fly!

A LOAD OF HOT AIR QUIZ

1 What is the name of the Chinese general who first used kites in warfare?

2 Have piloted ornithopter flights ever been successful?

3 In what year did Bartolomeu de Gusmao first demonstrate his hot-air balloon to the king and queen of Portugal?

4 Does hot air rise or fall?

5 Why does hot air rise?

6 Who was responsible for the first successful piloted hot-air balloon flight?

7 Who piloted the first balloon flight ever?

8 Who was the first pilot to die in an air disaster?

9 How dumb is it to try and fly a balloon that is a combined hot-air and hydrogen balloon?

10 Which Wright brother was Wilbur and which one was Orville?

11 December 17, 1903 is an important date in the history of flight. What happened on that day?

12 Have you finished this quiz?

ANSWERS

1 General Han Hsin.

2 Yes. In Russia in the 1990s successful piloted ornithopter flights were carried out.

3 1709.

4 It rises. That's why hot-air balloons go up rather than down. It is also why you never hear much of cold-air balloons.

5 The hot air is less dense than the cold air surrounding it and so is pushed upwards. Why? It just is!!! OK?

6 Frenchmen Joseph and Étienne Montgolfier in 1783.

7 A sheep, a duck and a rooster. I am not sure what the duck and rooster were doing there, seeing they had wings already.

8 François de Rozier. But what was he thinking, flying around in a flaming hot-air balloon with an explosive hydrogen balloon tied above it?

9 Very dumb.

10 That's easy! Wilbur was Wilbur and Orville was Orville.

11 The Wright brothers first achieved sustained, controlled and powered flight at a place called Kitty Hawk, North Carolina. It was the birth of the airplane.

12 Yes.

Timeline

1000 BC Chinese invent kites

1709 Bartolomeu de Gusmao demonstrates the first hot-air balloon

1783 Montgolfier brothers' first manned balloon flight

1785 First crossing of the English Channel in a hot-air balloon

1797 André-Jacques Garnerin's first descent by parachute

1799 George Cayley's concept drawing of a fixed-wing aircraft

1809 George and Sarah Cayley fly the first working model glider

1853 First manned glider flight by George Cayley's coachman

1884 Horatio Phillips designs the curved airfoil wing

1903 The first manned, powered and controlled flight in a heavier-than-air craft

1909 Louis Blériot is first to fly an airplane across the English Channel

1928 Amelia Earhart is the first woman to fly solo across the Atlantic Ocean

1928 Kingsford-Smith and Ulm fly across the Pacific Ocean

1931 Frank Whittle designs the first jet engine

1933 A Boeing 247 begins the first passenger flights

1939 Igor Sikorsky designs and flies the first helicopter

1942 World's first jet fighter, the *Messerschmitt 262*

1942 V2 makes first ever rocket flight

1957 Russians launch first Earth satellite, *Sputnik 1*

1959 Russian *Luna 2* lands on the moon

1963 First helicopter flight

1969 Armstrong and Aldrin are first men to walk on the moon

1979 Gossamer Albatross first man-powered aircraft to cross English Channel

1980 Flight of first solar-powered plane

2003 100 years since the Wright brothers' first flight

Glossary

ballast heavy material, like sandbags, carried in a balloon to allow the pilot to control its height

center of gravity the point on an object where its weight is balanced equally all around it

dihedral wing a wing shaped with an upward "vee"

fixed wing nearly all airplanes have wings fixed in position. Most wings have moving flaps that help steer the plane. Some military planes have wings that swing in and become smaller when the pilot wants to fly at faster speeds.

flapping flight birds and many insects fly by flapping their wings. Some early airplanes tried to imitate this action.

gondola the basket that hangs underneath a balloon. It carries the pilots, passengers, any equipment, gas cylinders and ballast.

heavier-than-air craft airplanes, because they are made of wood or metal, are heavier than air. They rely on their engines and wings to generate enough lift to make them fly.

helium gas helium is used in ballooning because it is the second lightest gas next to hydrogen. It is an inert gas, which means it won't explode and is very safe.

hydrogen the lightest of all gases, hydrogen is very explosive. While it was used in early ballooning, it was soon considered too dangerous and replaced by helium.

lift the combination of a plane's engine speed and wing shape provides the lift that allows it to fly

lighter-than-air craft balloons are filled with large volumes of hot air or light gas that makes them lighter than air and allows them to float in the air

ornithopters machines that fly using flapping wings

thrust the power of an engine that pushes the plane forward

wingspan the length of an aircraft's wing, measured from tip to tip

Where to find out more

Digital sources

Ornithopters

- www.ornithopter.org/birdflight

History of kites

- www.skratch-pad.com/kites/history.html
- www.users.voicenet.com/~foster/kites/page2.htm

Hot-air balloons

- http://travel.howstuffworks.com/hot-air-balloon.htm

Fixed-wing gliders

- http://wings.avkids.com/Book/History/instructor/gliders-01.html

The Wright brothers

- www.wam.umd.edu/~stwright/WrBr/taleplane.html
- www.wam.umd.edu/~stwright/WrBr/Wrights.html
- www.nasm.si.edu/wrightbrothers

History of flight

- www.ueet.nasa.gov/StudentSite/historyofflight.html

Microsoft *Encarta*

Books

Mary Kay Carson. *The Wright Brothers for Kids.* Chicago: Chicago Review Press, 2003.

Russell Freedman. *The Wright Brothers: How They Invented the Airplane.* New York: Holiday House, 1991.

T. A. Heppenheimer. *A Brief History of Flight.* New York: John Wiley & Sons, 2001.

David Macaulay. *The Way Things Work.* Boston: Houghton Mifflin, 1988.

Judith E. Rinard. *Book of Flight, The Smithsonian National Air and Space Museum.* New York: Firefly Books, 2001.

Index

About the author

TERRY DENTON dreamed of flying as a child. That's why he fell out of bed a lot. He and his brother used to make planes in the backyard. The cockpit was a wooden apple box and the wings were palings they pulled off the fence. Not only didn't these planes fly but their chickens escaped into the neighbor's veggie garden.

One day he made an ornithopter and tested it by jumping off his extremely high roof. Is it possible that he actually managed to fly? Of course not— he died a horrible and painful death. His ghost wrote and illustrated this book.

Thanks

The publishers would like to thank the following for photographs used in the text: Z Aviation Photos (Tony Zeljeznjak) for the photo of the replica *Wright Flyer* on page i, and istockphoto.com for the photo on page viii.